W
$13.95-03

Building Tools

By Inez Snyder

Welcome
Books

Children's Press®
A Division of Scholastic Inc.
New York / Toronto / London / Auckland / Sydney
Mexico City / New Delhi / Hong Kong
Danbury, Connecticut

Photo Credits: Maura B. McConnell
Contributing Editor: Jennifer Silate
Book Design: Daniel Hosek

Library of Congress Cataloging-in-Publication Data

Snyder, Inez.
Building tools / by Inez Snyder.
    p. cm. -- (Tools)
Includes bibliographical references and index.
Summary: A young boy and his father uses some simple tools to build a bookcase.
  ISBN 0-516-23976-7 (lib. bdg.) -- ISBN 0-516-24034-X (pbk.)
    1. Carpentry—Tools—Juvenile literature. 2. Bookcases—Juvenile literature. [1. Carpentry—Tools.] I.
    Title. II. Series.

TT197.5.B6 .S64 2002
684.1'6--dc21

2001053778

Contents

1 Tape Measure   6

2 Saw   12

3 Hammer and Nails   16

4 New Words   22

5 To Find Out More   23

6 Index   24

7 About the Author   24

My name is Andy.

Today, I am going to help my dad build a **bookcase**.

We will use many tools to build the bookcase.

5

This is a **tape measure**.

It is used to **measure** how long something is.

25′

33-425
MADE IN U.S.A.

7

This piece of wood has to be 20 **inches** long.

We measure the wood with the tape measure.

Dad uses a pencil to mark where he will cut.

We are ready to cut the wood.

Dad and I put on **safety glasses**.

They will keep our eyes safe.

This is a **saw**.

The saw is very sharp.

12

13

Dad uses the saw to cut the wood.

He cuts the wood on the mark he made.

15

This is a **hammer** and some **nails**.

A hammer is used to hit nails into wood.

17

Dad hits each nail into the wood.

The nails hold the pieces of wood together.

19

The bookcase is finished!

We used many tools
to build it.

21

New Words

bookcase (**buk**-kayss) a piece of furniture with shelves for holding books

hammer (**ham**-ur) a tool with a metal head fastened to a handle

inches (**inch**-iz) units of length equal to one-twelfth of a foot

measure (**mezh**-ur) to find the size of something

nails (**naylz**) slender pointed pieces of metal with flat or rounded tops, used to hold wood together

safety glasses (**sayf**-tee **glass**-iz) a glass or plastic covering that keeps eyes safe when working around dangerous things

saw (**saw**) a tool made of a thin, metal blade with sharp teeth on the edge for cutting

tape measure (**tayp mezh**-ur) a long strip of cloth or steel marked in inches and feet for measuring something

To Find Out More

Books
Building Machines and What They Do
by Derek Radford
Candlewick Press

Tool Book
by Gail Gibbons
Holiday House

Web Site
B4UBUILD.COM: Stuff 4 Kids
http://www.b4ubuild.com/kids/index.html
Play a word search puzzle, read about fun building projects, and more on this site.

Index

bookcase, 4, 20

hammer, 16

inches, 8

nail, 16, 18

pencil, 8

safety glasses, 10

saw, 12, 14

tape measure, 6, 8

wood, 8, 10, 14, 16, 18

About the Author
Inez Snyder writes and edits children's books. She also enjoys painting and cooking for her family.

Reading Consultants
Kris Flynn, Coordinator, Small School District Literacy, The San Diego County Office of Education

Shelly Forys, Certified Reading Recovery Specialist, W.J. Zahnow Elementary School, Waterloo, IL

Sue McAdams, Former President of the North Texas Reading Council of the IRA, and Early Literacy Consultant, Dallas, TX